I am grateful to God for everything! And I believe that the meaning of life is to make sense of other lives.

Fernanda Gouvea

2024

This Book Belongs to:

_____

F.G.P.©
all rights reserved

ALL RIGHTS RESERVED©
2024

No part of this publication may be reproduced, distributed, or transmitted in any form or by any means, including photocopying, recording, or other electronic or mechanical methods, without the prior written permission of the publisher, except for brief quotations incorporated in critical reviews and other specific noncommercial uses. Any unauthorized replica of this work is prohibited.

F.G.P.©
Fernanda Gouvea publications

Test Color Page

www.ingramcontent.com/pod-product-compliance
Lightning Source LLC
Chambersburg PA
CBHW062117220526
45471CB00010B/3774